The Hawaii Fact & Picture Book

By: Gina McIntyre

Introduction

Hawaii is one of the 50 states in the United States of America. The beautiful state of Hawaii is split into 67 counties. Let's explore the wonderful world of Hawaii!

Where is Hawaii Located?

Hawaii is an island state located in the Pacific Ocean, off the southwestern mainlands of the United States of America (USA). The USA is located in North America, in the Western hemisphere of the earth.

What States Border Hawaii?

Hawaii is is not bordered by any other states because it is an Island. Instead, Hawaii shares a coastline with the Pacific Ocean.

How Big is Hawaii?

Hawaii is the 47th largest state by area in the USA. It measures over 10,931 sq. miles, which is rather small in comparison to the other states. How big is your homeland?

What is the Population of Hawaii?

Hawaii is not heavily populated as it is quite small. An estimated 1.3 million people live in Hawaii.

When did Hawaii Become a State?

Hawaii became a state on August 21, 1959. At the time of statehood Hawaii became the 50th state of the USA.

Who Were the Original Settlers of Hawaii?

The first people to reach the Hawaiian Islands were the Polynesians of the Marquesas Islands. It was somewhere between A.D 300 to 600, when the Polynesians made their journey to the Islands.

What Types of Animals Live in Hawaii?

Hawaii is home to many unique animals, thanks to it's location in the Pacific Ocean. In Hawaii you can find Hawaiian Monk seals, Northern elephant seals, whales, dolphins, bats, an Indian Mongoose, feral wallabies, sheep, cats, dogs, and more!

Does Hawaii Have a Nickname?

Hawaii is called the aloha state. The abbreviation for Hawaii is HI. Does your homeland have a nickname?

What is the Hawaiian State Motto?

The state motto of Hawaii is "Ua mau ke ea o ka aina i ka pono." Translated, it means "The life of the land is perpetuated in righteousness."

What does the Hawaiian State Flag Look Like?

The Hawaiian state flag features a Union Jack flag in the upper left hand corner, with 8 horizontal stripes throughout the rest of the flag. Those red, white, and blue stripes were added in 1816 in order to make a distinctive flag for Hawaii.

What is the State Flower of Hawaii?

The state flower of Hawaii is the hibiscus. The Hawaiian hibiscus flowers bloom almost every day, but they only last for a day or so before dying.

What is the State Tree of Hawaii?

The state tree of Hawaii is called the Kukui or candlenut tree. The Kukui tree became the official state tree of Hawaii on May 1,1959.

What is the Capital of Hawaii?

The capital of Hawaii is Honolulu. Honolulu is located on the island of Oahu.

What Types of Food are Popular in Hawaii?

Many of Hawaii's traditional food dishes are recipes passed on or brought over from the Pacific Polynesian islands. Here are a few of the most loved traditional dishes: poi, laulau, kalua pig, poke, lomi salmon, chicken long rice, and fruit like pineapple!

Does Hawaii Have a State Dance?

Yes! The state dance of Hawaii is the hula dance. The hula dance was once only used for special ceremonies, now it is used as a form of entertainment.

What Language is Spoken in Hawaii?

The official language of the US and Hawaii is English. However, Hawaiian and Hawaiian Pidgin English are also considered official languages of Hawaii.

What is the Highest Point in Hawaii?

The highest point in Hawaii is called Mauna Kea, it is located on the Island of Hawaii. Mauna Kea stands an estimated 13,803 feet tall.

What is the Geography in Hawaii?

The state of Hawaii is actually a chain of islands, 132 of them to be exact! Some islands consist of rock while others consists of coral and sand. Approximately 124 of the 132 islands are not suitable for people to live on.

Does Hawaii Have a National Park?

Yes, Hawaii is home to two national parks. They are called Haleakala National Park and Hawaii Volcanoes National Park.

What is a Volcano?

A volcano looks like a big mountain or hill. It has a large crater, or vent, that often spews lava, rock fragment and other dangerous gases from the Earth's crust.

Made in the USA
Lexington, KY
14 March 2018